for . . . .

· for your birthday ·

by

Lauren White

Sourcebooks, Inc.
Naperville, IL

BIRTHDAY RECIPE
· leisurely breakfast ·

plump pillows

orange juice

hot coffee

marmalade

fresh flowers

plus

birthday cards to open

birthday treats Nº1

dancing

on the tabletop

BIRTHDAYS

TO

OPPORTUNITY

ARE

WATCH

AN

YOURSELF

CHANGING

AND

GROWING

B I R T H D A Y

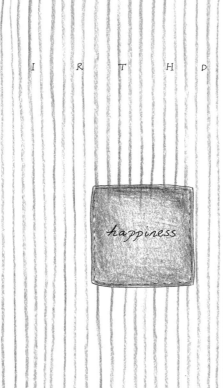

happiness

monday's child is fair of face......

tuesday's child is full of grace.

wednesday's child is full of woe....

thursday's child has far to go.

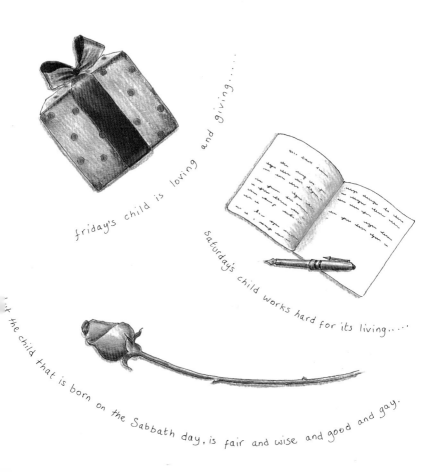

friday's child is loving and giving.....

saturday's child works hard for its living.....

..t the child that is born on the Sabbath day, is fair and wise and good and gay.

BIRTHDAY RECIPE
· birthday card ·

special message

thoughtful design

stamps

envelope

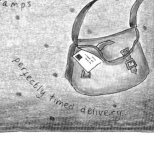

perfectly timed delivery

birthday treats №2

eating

whatever you fancy

WE

THE

AGE

OUTSIDE

MAY

ON

INSIDE

THE

JUST

SAME

BUT

WE'RE

B I R T H D A Y

health

BIRTHDAY RECIPE
· ideal morning ·

newspapers

big pot of tea

biscuits

birthday messages

a bit of shopping

plus

sunshine

birthday treats Nº3

drinking

to the good health of your loved ones

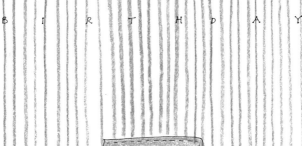

B I R T H D A Y

peace

january ~ snowdrop

february ~ primrose

march ~ violet

april ~ daisy

may ~ hawthorn

june ~ wild rose

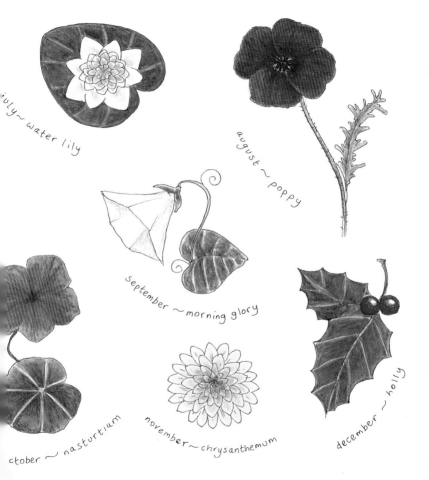

july ~ water lily

august ~ poppy

september ~ morning glory

october ~ nasturtium

november ~ chrysanthemum

december ~ holly

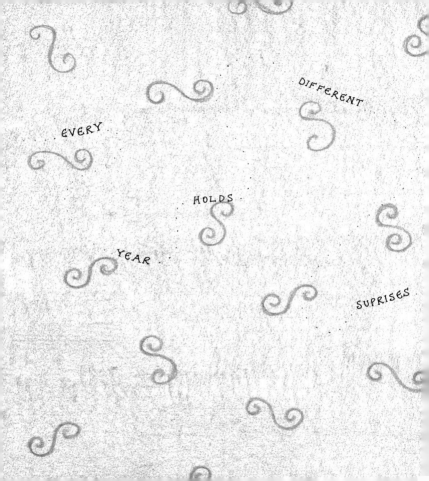

EVERY

DIFFERENT

HOLDS

YEAR

SUPRISES

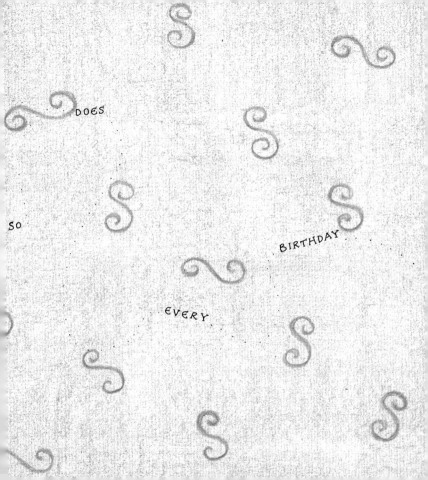

DOES

SO

BIRTHDAY

EVERY

wealth

BIRTHDAY RECIPE
· perfect wrapping ·

string

scissors

label

wrapping paper

ribbon

birthday treats №4

wishing

for heaven on earth!

BIRTHDAYS ARE A CHANCE

TO

LIFE

CELEBRATE

...A · DAY · TO ...

eat fantastic amounts of chocolate

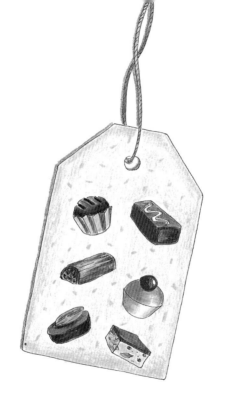

B I R T H D A Y

may your dreams
come true

plus

peace and quiet

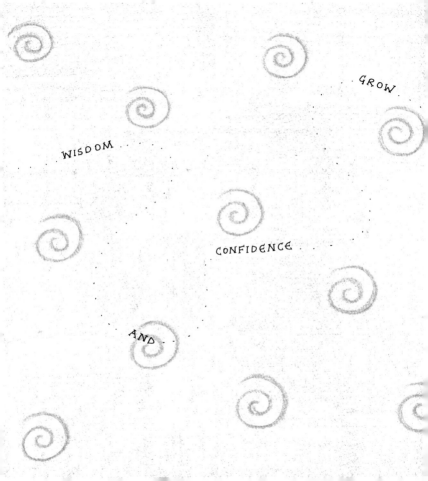

GROW

WISDOM

CONFIDENCE

AND

YEAR

YEAR...

BY

birthday treats N°5

singing

happy birthday to me

...A · DAY · TO...

Stand on your head

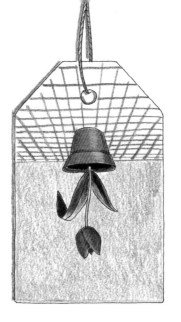

W I S H E S N° VI

BIRTHDAY RECIPE
• lazy afternoon •

wine

sunshine

deckchairs

bread and cheese

sunglasses

add

good conversation

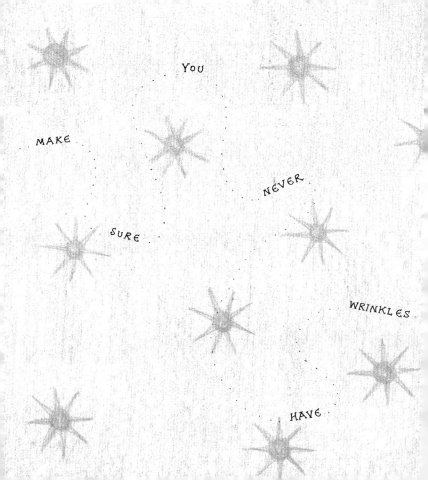

YOU

MAKE

NEVER

SURE

WRINKLES

HAVE

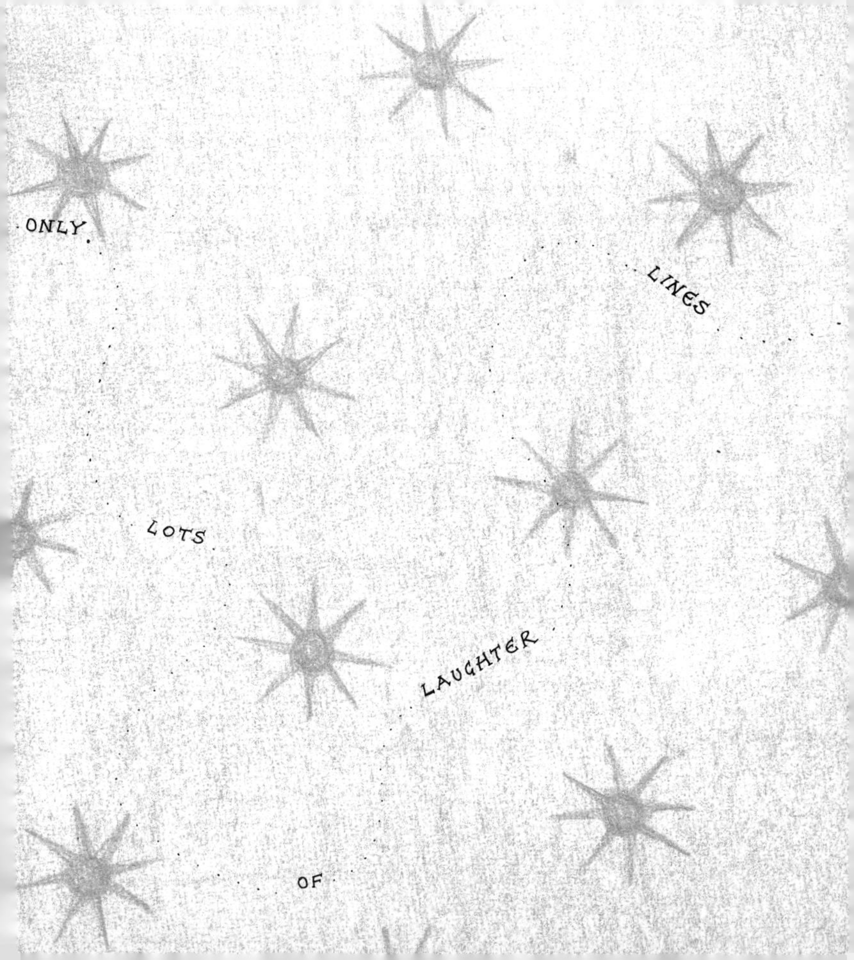

ONLY

LINES

LOTS

LAUGHTER

OF

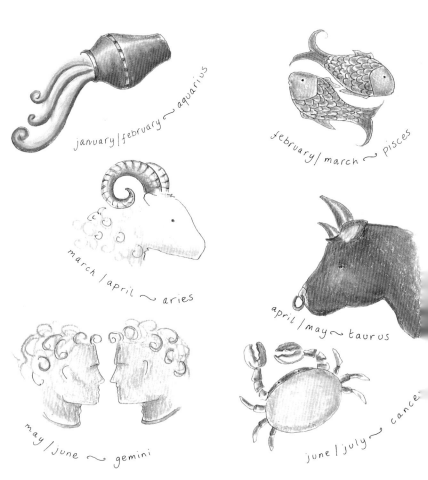

january/february ~ aquarius

february/march ~ pisces

march/april ~ aries

april/may ~ taurus

may/june ~ gemini

june/july ~ cancer

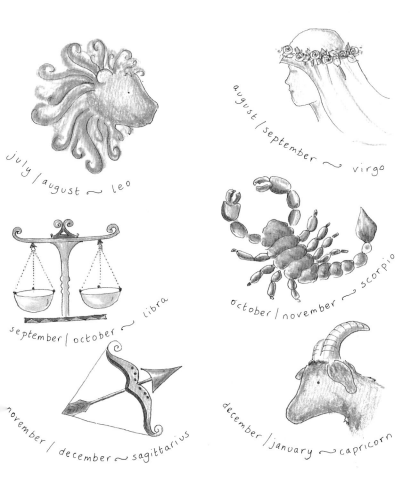

july / august ~ leo

august / september ~ virgo

september / october ~ libra

october / november ~ scorpio

november / december ~ sagittarius

december / january ~ capricorn

BIRTHDAY

time to fulfil
your ambitions

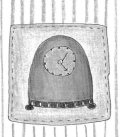

...A · DAY · TO ...

give

someone

a

BIG

hug

birthday treats N°6

laughing

and having fun with good friends

BIRTHDAY RECIPE
·cake·

big mixing bowl

wooden spoon

currants

'icing

candles

BIRTHDAY

18TH

ON   SUPPOSED

YOUR

YOU'RE

TO

40TH

ON

YOUR

YOU'RE

GROWN-UP

NOT!

BE

BIRTHDAY RECIPE
· afternoon tea ·

buttered scones

tea

linen napkins

sandwiches

cream

strawberry jam

B I R T H D A Y

breakfast   lunch

C A K E

supper

"just a little piece before bed..."

ON

YOUR BIRTHDAY

WHAT

YOU

SAY

DO

CAN

AND

OU

WANT

TAKE

THE

OPPORTUNITY!

...A · DAY · TO ...

have a teddy bears picnic!

BIRTHDAY RECIPE
· party ·

jelly

silly hats

cake

lemonade

presents

BIRTHDAYS

ARE

CHANCE

A

LOOK

TO

WHERE

AT

GOING

YOUR

IS

LIFE

birthday treats №7

dressing

in your "birthday best"

BIRTHDAY RECIPE
birthday bathtime

candles

big bath

fragrant oils

soft music

fluffy robe

BIRTHDAY

friendship

EACH

BIRTHDAY

YOUR

IS

PERSONAL

DAY

YEAR'S

NEW

birthday treats Nº8

sharing

all the joy of the day

BIRTHDAY RECIPE
·candlelit dinner·

velvet sky

moonlight

cocktails

lipstick

good food

...A · DAY · TO...

make one personal wish

january ~ garnet ~ constancy

february ~ amethyst ~ sincerity

march ~ bloodstone ~ bravery

april ~ diamond ~ innocence

may ~ emerald ~ happiness

june ~ pearl ~ health

july ~ ruby ~ love

august ~ sardonyx ~ luck

september ~ sapphire ~ wisdom

october ~ opal ~ hope

...mber ~ topaz ~ fidelity

december ~ turquoise ~ success

B I R T H D A Y

laughter

W I S H E S Nº IX

AGE

A

IS

STATE OF MIND

BIRTHDAY RECIPE
· indulgence ·

champagne

peeled grapes

big cosy armchair

handmade chocolates

and

plenty of time

BIRTHDAY

fun

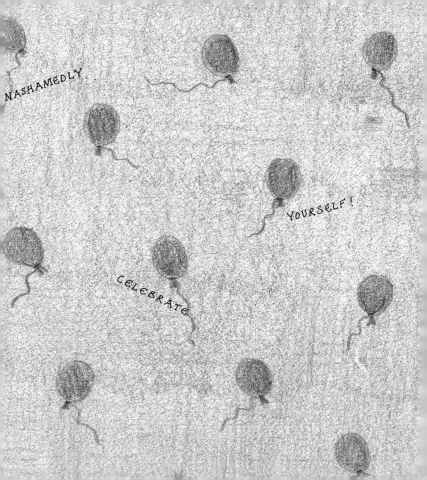

happy birthday

"Adding a sprinkling of magic to the everyday..." is how Lauren White describes her original style of drawing. Born and brought up in the village of Cranfield in Bedfordshire County, England, she studied fine art in Hull and London before returning to Bedfordshire to work as resident illustrator for a local wildlife trust. Lauren loves playing the piano, walking her dog Jack, and she carries a sketchbook everywhere she goes. She lives with her partner, Michael, and describes herself as having an astonishing collection of marbles and a wicked sense of humor. Lauren's designs for Hotchpotch greetings cards are sold around the world, and in this book she continues to refine her distinctive style which "celebrates the simple things in life."

other titles in this series:

Friends
Home Sweet Home
Baby

Published in 2000 by
Sourcebooks, Inc
1935 Brookdale Road, Suite 139
Naperville IL 60563

Copyright © MQ Publications Limited 2000

Text & Illustrations © Lauren White 2000
Printed and bound in Italy

MQ 10 9 8 7 6 5 4 3 2 1

ISBN: 1-57071-521-1